My Crazy Brooklyn Stories

Whims, Woes, and Cappuccinos

Christina Rivera

Copyright © 2024. CHRISTINA Rivera.
All rights reserved.

My Crazy Brooklyn Stories
Whims, Woes, and Cappuccinos

written by Christina Rivera.

CrazyNestCreations.etsy.com

Photographs and illustrations were created by
Bryan C. Rivera and Christina Rivera.

Edited and carefully proofread by Bryan C. Rivera.

No part of this book may be reproduced or used in any way without the written permission of the copyright owner.

ISBN: 9798336201772

Dedication

Thank you Lord God our Father, Jesus, and Holy Spirit
for your wonderful blessings and for empowering me with life,
many unique gifts, and many talents.
Your servant awaits your return.

I also thank my beautiful and spectacularly talented husband,
Bryan
for his support and skill in designing our illustrations, diligent
proofreading, and editing our inspirational book.

Thank you, Mr. Henry F. Hobbs
for your friendship and companionship.
Stay furry, hombre!

Thank you, Doc
for introducing to us New Yorkers
the Texas Lone Star State experience.
The Republic lives!

"But as it is written, Eye hath not seen, nor ear heard, neither
have entered into the heart of man, the things which God hath
prepared for them that love him."
I Corinthians 2:9 KJV

Table of Contents

Chapter 1: New Neighborhood Shenanigans 7
Chapter 2: Washroom Warfare 11
Chapter 3: Toraji's Midnight Departure 15
Chapter 4: Sydney's Senior Tuxedo 22
Chapter 5: Feline Frenzy 26
Chapter 6: The Norwegian Forest 31
Chapter 7: Fur-ever Friend 35
Chapter 8: Thousand-dollar Scone 42
Chapter 9: Cappuccino Chronicles 47
Chapter 10: Snowed-in Smart Summer Ale 53
Chapter 11: Brooklyn Heights, Texas Delights 58

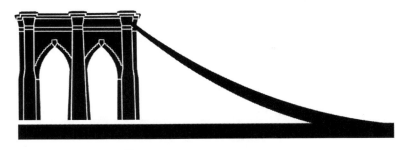

Chapter 1
New Neighborhood Shenanigans

This story begins where my last one ended with, *My Crazy Roommates*. After finally leaving the world of roommates behind, I found an awesome solo apartment in Bay Ridge, Brooklyn. It was a 14 year escapade of fun and humor in the best borough of the Big Apple, Brooklyn!

Having lived with roommates for many years, I usually used their furniture and had very little of my own when I moved into my new digs. My boyfriend, and later husband, nearly passed out when he walked into our new apartment. Having lived in houses his whole life, this 374-square-foot apartment was like moving into a closet. Bry quickly sat down to catch his breath, while I ordered sushi for our dinner. Sushi had a way of making everything better!

As we unpacked, our next door neighbor, Edward came over and introduced himself. "I just wanted to come over and meet my new neighbors," he said. All the neighbors seemed delighted. Most were retired and over the age of

65. Sadly, many original tenants passed away over the next few years. It was like living in a retirement home where elderly tenants were checkin' out faster than new tenants checkin' in!

One evening, not too many months after moving in, we heard a frantic knock at our door. It was a brother and sister who anxiously told us their dad lived below our apartment. Before reaching our apartment, they knocked on his dad's apartment door for several minutes without getting a response. They were trying to get in touch with him for many days without any success. The brother asked if he could pass through our window onto the fire escape and descend to his father's place to see if pop was okay.

A few minutes later, the sad reality was revealed when the brother screamed up to us! He saw his dad on the floor, unresponsive. He managed to get into the apartment by violently tearing away the air conditioner unit from the window. When inside, they called 911 for their dad who was already dead.

In addition to elderly neighbors, we had the best superintendent. He was a bit annoying when it came to building maintenance. Jerry acted like it was his home while taking great care of the property and tenants. He, of course, expected all residents to be considerate by contributing to the care and condition of our building. I didn't mind his hounding; because if we all did our part, the building would remain in tip-top shape for all of us.

I remember the day I moved in. Jerry reminded me to cover 80 percent of the floor with a rug or carpet as stipulated by the contract. I told him our rugs and new furniture were on the way and should arrive within a day or two. Jerry, a Guatemalan immigrant who spoke with a strong Spanish accent had a saying, "Do you wanna be especial?" This meant you didn't wanna be on his naughty neighbor list!

Jerry once shared a story on how the FDNY was very "especial" when they responded to a reported gas leak in our building. The fire-fighters arrived jacked up and ready to bust open the door. He tried getting them to chill out for a moment while he quickly ran down to his office to get the key, but they carried on and brutally axed the door wide open!

Our neighborhood was a wonderful place to live in with most of our tenants being super friendly. Next door was a Catholic church; and throughout the day we'd hear soothing church bells gently chiming each hour.

Our building was originally designed and built to be a hotel during the early part of the 20th century. It had an ornate water fountain on display within the main lobby. Since the fountain was antiquated and decommissioned, it was repurposed with a decorative faux-plant and white gravel arrangement inside the base of the pool. There were two comfy padded chairs strategically placed on each side of the lobby with small beverage tables. Tenants and guests lounged in this common area to socialize, read, relax, or wait for rides.

Inside our lobby of highly polished stone floor-tiles was a larger table. It was positioned in front of a huge painting against the main wall next to the elevator. There, many of our fellow tenants would give away a variety of personal items. They gifted our community with things like cookies and pastries, canned goods, flatware, clothing, books and magazines. Occasionally there would be small furnishings like lamps, fans, mirrors, and picture frames. It was like a communal treasure hunt. One tenant's cupcake was another tenant's free breakfast pastry!

So, it began! My journey through Brooklyn was filled with quirky characters, unexpected events, and many laughs along the way. If there was one thing my Brooklyn guaranteed, it made sure inner-city life was always exciting!

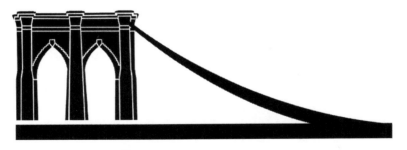

Chapter ❷
Washroom Warfare

Of all the apartment buildings I lived in across the five boroughs of New York City, Jerry stood out as the best superintendent. Any service call was immediately addressed and resolved usually within the hour for minor issues and within the week for complicated ones.

In rare instances when our elevator was out of service, Jerry set up metal folding chairs on each of the stairwell floor landings. He made sure the elderly residents could rest between floors on the way up or down if needed. Jerry also went the extra mile by offering assistance to elderly tenants by volunteering to pick up grocery items from the store. Honestly, I imagined him offering piggyback rides up the stairs. He probably would have done it!

Jerry was a kind man who took his responsibilities as a super seriously. Some of our residents took offense at his active commitment to perfection in managing the building. Despite the occasional criticism, I never took offense at

Jerry's recommendations because I saw he genuinely had the best interests of all residents at heart. Jerry served as an experienced building superintendent for over 18 years when I first moved in.

Interestingly, one of our neighbors who rented an apartment on the first floor, Carol, lived in our building since childhood. As a child, her father was in charge of our building for many years before Jerry was hired as a replacement. Most neighbors were elderly and very friendly, but not Carol! She invoked unmerited special privileges as royal princess of the building, heir apparent of her father's past kingdom as superintendent.

Our basement housed the laundry room and it contained three washers and three dryers for our multi-unit six-floored building. At the other end of the basement, was a small room with a separate washer and dryer reserved for the use of the royal family. Since Carol's dad was super many years ago, she kept a copy of his master key. Because of this, her family never surrendered their keys to the owner of the property.

Often, princess Carol descended from her self-assumed throne with stacks of laundry. She not only filled the separate machine in the super's laundry room, but all three washers in the main laundry room. If any of the building's subjects removed her clothes from any of the machines after their completed wash-cycles, she raged! If she was unreasonably late to unload the machines, she flipped out when the unclean touched her royal threads. Knowing how terribly difficult she was, I avoided the scene when she was in the laundry room. Princess wasn't worth my time; so I came back another day to wash my garments in peace.

One evening, I came down to the laundry room and saw only one washer occupied. Great, I'll use the other two. This should be enough to clean all of my laundry. I gathered my clothes, loaded the washers, and went upstairs to start my weekend cleaning and cooking. Half hour later, I returned to the basement to unload the washers when I noticed Carol there. I said a cheerful hello and walked over to the machines.

Without my permission, Carol emptied both of my machines and scattered my laundry haphazardly on a nearby table! Okay, no worries, I thought. I'll just load them into both dryers and come back in 30 minutes.

When I went to load my clothes into one of the dryers, I noticed all three dryers had six quarters sitting in their coin-slots. It was then, Carol informed me all these dryers were hers and was holding them for her wet clothes. "Huh?" I looked over and saw Carol's three washing machines running. "You can't hold the dryers," I said. "You still have 25 minutes to go on your wash-cycles." Carol replied with, "I have a lot of laundry and you'll just have to wait."

At this moment, a different tenant from the first washing machine entered the laundry room. After hearing our conversation, she went into a full-fledged scream fest. The first tenant said she was there before any of us arrived and needed all three dryers. She wanted to dry her clothes separately according to garment type. I wondered why on Earth would she need three dryers? In reality, since all of her clothes were being washed in one machine, only one dryer was required.

While the two of them hysterically went at each other's throats, I noticed clothes-lines in the back of the room for tenants to hang-dry their laundry. I used most of the lines for my two machines of wet clothing. After all was completed, I turned around and thanked both of them for saving me five dollars! Weeks after that emotionally-charged incident, all of us got along well in our building.

As years passed, many of our sweet elderly residents died while new younger neighbors moved in to occupy the available apartments. Because Jerry carefully vetted potential renters, all new folks were as pleasant and considerate as the prior ones. Unfortunately, about seven years down the road, many things changed. More about that, in another chapter.

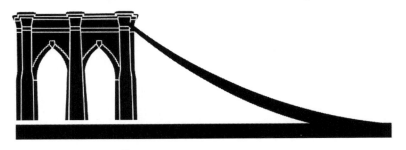

Chapter ❸
Toraji's Midnight Departure

After our building was sold. year seven brought a change in management. Sadly, Jerry was released and required to move within a few months. His replacement superintendent, Joe, turned out to be the worst super I had the displeasure of knowing. Joe was rarely on-scene, leaving residents to figure out solutions when something in their apartments broke. There was only one positive thing which came from the switch; pets were allowed. Yay!

Reflecting on my childhood, I remember Rexie our amazing German Shepherd. She was the loyal companion I grew up with. So loyal, she guarded my room like an armed soldier on duty from the day I was brought home from the hospital.

My mom shared a story of how at three years old, I wandered away from the house to a nearby highway in Arlington, Virginia. As we walked together, Rexie strategically positioned herself on my left, shielding me from traffic. Because of this bizarre scene of a child and a dog walking alone by the side of a dangerously busy road, a kind police officer saw us, stopped, and brought us home in his cruiser.

With these cherished memories of Rexie over the past couple of years, I had a strong desire to have my own dog. However, Bryan, my partner and future husband, was against having a dog in our humble abode. Because of Bry's upbringing with dogs in the backyard, he believed animals should be outdoors and not share indoor living spaces with humans.

Hmmm, how could I convince Bry about having our very own Yorkie? It was around this time I discovered a cool new cat care service which set up cat owners with vetted people to shelter their cats while they were away. Most contracts were one week to six months. In some rare cases, a full year of housing could be arranged. The cat owner paid sitters to house, feed, and care for their furry friends. This was the perfect solution! While getting Bry used to the excitement of indoor pet ownership, we'd make extra cash. This was a win for us both.

I called the kitty service to book an in-home meeting where the company reviewed our home making sure it was pet safe. My vetting process went well. Within the next two weeks, I received my first contract with them.

One owner was looking to move to Japan and needed us to watch their beautiful Bengal cat named Torji for one year. Torji was on the older side. He was about ten years old with a sweet and friendly disposition.

Toraji was a rescue kitty. His owner Sarah, didn't know his previous history. Since poor old Toraji was a fearful little guy, instead of hanging out on top of things, he spent most of his time hiding under things. He spent many hours under our bed and armoire. After a couple of weeks, Torji, as we called him, became more comfortable with us and came out when we arrived home from work. After our initial brief moment of bonding, he let us pet and play with him.

I prepared Toraji's food while Bryan gave him a firm and relatively aggressive massage which Torji loved. This was odd because many cats usually don't like being over stimulated. I was known as the feeder and Bry the master masseur.

During one hot summer night, we kept the apartment door wide open for cross ventilation. After cleaning up the dinner dishes and getting ready for bed, I closed the door. Later, I kneeled to look under the bed where Torji hid to wish him goodnight. He wasn't there. Okay, he must be under the armoire. I looked under it and he wasn't there either. I became nervous and told Bry I couldn't find Toraji.

Our tiny 374 square-foot Brooklyn apartment didn't provide many places for a kitty to hide. We quickly descended into panic-mode after checking all possible hiding places in our apartment. Initially, we weren't worried about Torji sneaking out for a tour of the building since he was a fearful cat. We assumed he passed through the doorway when we weren't looking. We had to find him immediately! Thinking about telling Sarah I lost her beloved pet during the middle of the night tormented me.

There were six floors in our building with two stairwells at opposite ends of the hallway. Bry and I independently searched both stairwells up and down slowly, stopping at each flight shouting Toraji's name. After reaching the first floor, I looked under the stairs where Queen Carol hid her kids' toys, but I didn't see Torji there. I was annoyed seeing Carol's collection of things hidden under the steps because tenants weren't allowed to store personal property according to FDNY fire regulations. Any other tenant would have been in trouble with management, but not her.

Anyway, while searching for this missing cat, I suspected he was snatched by a neighbor. I suspected this because I recently began using a local delivery service to have my detergent, liquid soaps, and other assorted household products dropped off at my apartment door. I never had a problem with packages not being delivered until one day I was away at work.

When I returned to my apartment later in the evening, I saw the shipping box near my door ripped open. All of the items, about a hundred dollars worth, were gone except one. A box of sanitary pads was left inside and I suspected my next door neighbor took it. He was a much older fella who lived alone retired from U.S. military service.

He was usually drunk and at times made several failed flirtatious attempts to date me. Once he tried pushing me into his apartment saying, he wanted to show me something. After this scary event, I made sure not to walk close to his door or be in the same hallway with him. Over the following years of his excessive drinking, he was never safe to be around. If he was the alleged thief of my cheap household goods, which I suspected, how much more motivated would he be to snatch a purebred Bengal cat?!

At 2:00 am, exhausted and not knowing what else to do, I reluctantly knocked on my old military vet's apartment door. He opened and answered in a cloud of confusion rubbing his eyes, disturbed from sleep. Standing disoriented in his old man briefs, he abrasively and forcefully asked, "what do you want!?" I replied with, "do you have a cat?" He said, "yes, why?!" Without hesitation I fired with, "could I see him?!" He shot back with, "now?!" I said, "yes!"

Mind you, it was well past midnight and still hours away from sunrise. My neighbor didn't resist and went into the other room to fetch his cat. I began looking under all of his furniture, calling for Toraji. My neighbor came back a few minutes later with a cardboard box in his arms and an orange Tabby kitty in it. I immediately looked at the cat and exclaimed, "oh, ah, that's not him!"

Totally embarrassed, I followed with, "um, okay, sorry for waking you up and bothering you." It was then my neighbor's face changed. He clearly understood the jolting accusation presented before him and realized I believed HE was the cat burglar! Because of this, my neighbor cursed me out firing insults, and unspeakable profanities as I quickly bolted out of his apartment. His anger was warranted, but I was desperate! I would not sleep until we found Torji... hopefully alive!

There was no way I could go back to Sarah saying I lost her cat. She trusted me to take care of her special kitty so I decided to do one last desperate sweep of the building before searching outside.

I walked downstairs moving slowly and methodically through each floor. When I arrived at ground level where Carol hid her kid's toys under the stairwell, I looked again. Just when I was about to leave and search another floor, out of the corner of my eye I saw a flicker of green light. Hidden within the collection of toys was... Toraji! I crawled in and pulled him out. He was stiff as a board, paralyzed with fear!

I quickly held him in my arms and breathed a sigh of great relief as I cradled and carried him back to our apartment. We were so grateful Torji was safe and unhurt.

Sarah, Toraji's owner and I became good friends over the following years. Later, with the passing of time, I shared this near "cat-astrophic" event with her. All was forgiven since her beloved cat was doing well and she knew we loved him dearly. No matter how warm the apartment became with Toraji around, we'd never leave the apartment door wide open ever again.

One year flew by fast and soon it was time for Sarah to take Torji home. During the year, Torji and I became great friends. After Sarah arrived at the apartment, she prepped him for transport and began loading her cat into his carry box. While this was happening, he looked at me with confusion, uncertainty, and fear through his big beautiful eyes as if to say, "what did I do, why did you betray me?" I was in tears and the pain of separation was setting in. Sarah and I exchanged hugs and tearful goodbyes right before she walked out never to see our friend Toraji ever again.

A few short weeks later, Sarah contacted me and said they were having difficulties getting Torji's paperwork settled. In order to bring an animal to Japan, extensive special requirements must be met. All pets have to be micro-chipped, tested for rabies antibodies, vaccinated, and be subject to a 180-day waiting period before international transport. Sarah asked if I could keep him a bit longer as she worked to get things in order. Sarah cried saying she was scared. If this couldn't be resolved, she might have to abandon him at the local animal shelter.

I replied by saying, absolutely not! Toraji would not be left alone in a shelter! If by chance things didn't work out with the paperwork, we'd take Torji home with us. Sarah could visit him anytime she was in New York.

After Sarah successfully navigated two months of stress filled bureaucratic box-checking, the unreasonably exhaustive process finally ended. Thank God! In celebration, we threw a Brooklyn-styled bon voyage party with pizza and cocktails. This time... Torji left happily with his family. Since our moment with this wonderful Bengal cat gave us so many fond memories, I enthusiastically looked forward to our next cat adventure. We didn't have to wait long!

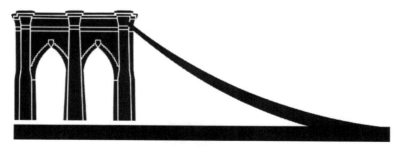

Chapter 4
Sydney's Senior Tuxedo

We received a call from Joe the kennel owner saying he had another contract he thought would be a great fit for us. An older cat named Sid, was a 20-year-old senior tuxedo cat, wow! This unique contract was open for a 6 month run. I was a little nervous about this commitment because this old fella had a high probability of dying in our care.

Joe comforted us by saying the owner understood the high risk and was willing to move forward by signing a no liability waiver. If Sid died, no legal action would be taken against us. I reluctantly agreed to meeting Sid's owner, River. She brought her cat and we had a lovely introduction. Sid seemed to be chill, and River was sweet. Just before leaving, she joked by saying, "No worries, I know my Sid is old. If he dies, just feel free to toss him in the freezer and I'll pick him up when I get back."

"What?!" I said, stunned.

"I'm just joking," she quipped.

"Hahaha," I thought, "not funny! I don't want a dead cat in my freezer!"

Since I could use the extra money, I signed the six-month contract to care for Sid.

All started off well for the first couple of days. River told us Sid liked going for walks each day on a leash. I thought it was strange taking a cat out for walks, but okay! This was a great way to get Bryan used to dog ownership one day.

We soon realized Sid was quite the demanding kitty! He wanted to go out for walks at random times of the day including waking us up in the middle of the night. Once it was around 4 a.m. when he put his mouth under the apartment's door and howled until one of us got up. I jumped out of bed to stop this crazy cat from waking up our neighbors with his persistent howls.

One early morning, I wasn't in the mood to go out for a pre-dawn excursion. Because of this, I decided to put Sid in our bathroom with his food and water so I could get back to bed. He continued howling and scratching at the bathroom door, but at least we were the only ones hearing him instead of the whole building.

The following morning I made my way towards the bathroom door to let Sidney out. Immediately after pushing the door open, Sid bolted out! While our guest cat was roaming around the apartment reorienting himself, I was in the kitchen preparing breakfast. Several minutes later, with breakfast complete, I spotted him lounging on our plush black sofa. I placed Sid's bowl of chow on the floor then walked over to cuddle with him a bit. At the moment I sat down on the couch, I noticed it was wet. What?! It was cat pee! He didn't just pee in one spot, Sid soaked the entire sofa was his ferociously pungent feline piss!

If you're not familiar with cat urine, the smell is nauseatingly noxious! No matter how aggressively I cleaned and disinfected our beautiful sofa, I just couldn't get rid of the horrible stench! On top of all that, Sid soaked the small cat bed I bought for him as a gift. Soon after, I called him "terror kitty." He had us well trained into kitty-compliance after this e-piss-ode.

We didn't want the rest of our tiny apartment to be destroyed! When he howled, we just took him outside for his walks. Sid, our little terror, was loads of work keeping him happy and this didn't help my case. Bry's argument against owning a household pet remained.

Sid and I eventually found equilibrium and became friends. He was an adventurous cat who loved exploring nature much like his owner, River. River traveled the world looking for the perfect wave to hang-ten while working out of her computer laptop as a movie editor. Because Sid was so old, it became difficult to travel with him or find people to care for him because he was such a handful. River loved her friend Sid, but was ready for him to climb towards kitty heaven.

One of the cool things we got to experience every morning was our kitty alarm clock. Sid jumped onto the bed and positioned his face an inch from his preferred human's face. When he was ready, he meowed loudly until someone woke up. Good morning!

I enjoyed walking in the park with our friend. In fact, the day River returned to pick up Sid, I was out at the park with him. When I returned, I saw River talking to Bry. She was happy knowing her little Sid was having a wonderful visit and enjoying his walks. I grew to love Sid, but was quite relieved when his owner took him back home. I was looking forward to getting a good night's rest.

After River left our apartment, we had a follow-up conversation a few days later over the phone. She asked how things worked out. I reluctantly replied with, Sidney peed the couch in an act of retaliation for locking him in the bathroom after meowing loudly during the middle of the night.

I didn't want to say anything about the couch when River came by since I was planning to get a new couch anyway. It wasn't a big deal. When River heard this, she was embarrassed and apologized. I said, no worries. A few days later, she surprised us by sending $200.00 for the damage via a cash app. That was unexpected, but it was greatly appreciated!

Living with Sid was challenging. Not all pet experiences turned out the way we expected them to. Many potential owners buy dogs and cats with certain expectations of what they think their relationship will be with their new pets. So, before getting a kitty or a doggie, understand it won't be easy. It's a never ending journey of love, patience, and personal sacrifice. Caring for a pet is an act of love until death.

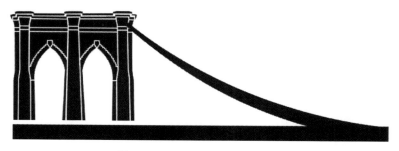

Chapter 5
Feline Frenzy

After Sid was gone, I wasn't in a rush to cat-sit anytime soon. Six months later, Joe contacted me with an awesome new gig. It was a short 3-day contract watching three cats. Easy-peasy, I thought. Boy, was I wrong!

I met the owner of the three cats at a local coffee shop near us. She lived about half a mile from me. Pat seemed nice. She said she was getting married in a couple of weeks and needed someone to watch her fur babies during the wedding and short honeymoon. After our initial meeting, Pat invited me back to her place to see the kitties.

When we arrived at her pad, the three cats were nowhere to be seen. After a few minutes they started coming out of their hiding places. Curiously and cautiously, they checked me out. The first two cats I was introduced to were Ace and Cookie.

Ace, the oldest was a light beige Tabby. Cookie, a black and white Tuxedo was a recent addition to the pride. They both were super sweet. Max, the third cat finally appeared, and he was not friendly. He immediately attacked his brother and sister. When he saw me, he welcomed me with a drive-by slashing.

Pat saw I was having second thoughts about taking care of her cats. She tried to convince me Max was a sweetheart. Once I got to know him, all would be well. She recommended I put lotion on my hands, wait for him to purr, then pet him. This was a strange tactic, but I went along with the program to see what could happen.

Max's owner excused herself to fetch some lotion. When she returned, Pat handed me the bottle. I lathered on a good amount of lotion while she picked Max up. Pat placed Max next to me and I cautiously petted his head. As soon as I began touching him, Max slashed my hand and ran to the other side of the room. Pat apologized profusely! She conveniently forgot to tell me Max didn't like his head being touched! If this cat stayed with me, I'd feed him and never go anywhere near this guy! I reluctantly agreed to watch her kitties. Did I make a mistake? I was about to find out soon.

A few weeks later, the day before kitty pick up, Pat called and asked if I'd take her cats the night before our official start. Since it was only an extra 12 hours, I agreed to do it.

After Pat arrived at my place with her three cats, she unloaded them from their carriers. As soon as they were set free, all three cats immediately bolted to separate corners of my apartment. While Pat unpacked their food and supplies, the feline tension was rapidly building. Things were shaping up to be a problem and it was obvious. I seriously wanted to shut the scene down by canceling, but I agreed to the terms. It was too late and Pat's wedding was the following evening. Contractually, I couldn't do anything about it. I tricked myself into believing I could totally handle a short three and a half days with these cats.

During the next few hours after Pat left, I regretted my assignment and I knew sleep was going to be difficult. If Ace and Cookie came out of their hiding places, Max would run out and pounce on them triggering an explosive cat fight! I wanted none of this. When it was time for bed, I decided to sleep with my comforter over my head. This was a great idea because during the night I felt cat paws running and leaping over my body while Max terrorized Ace and Cookie.

Next morning, my room was eerily quiet. Only one cat was spotted, Cookie, sitting on top of my armoire. Prepping for work, I wondered about surviving the next couple of days with my furry visitors. Maybe one of my friends would help by letting me crash on their couch during the next few days. If so, I'd come by every evening to make sure they were fed and their litter boxes cleaned.

Thinking about my plan, I walked towards the closet to pull out my clothes for the day. The moment I reached in, Max leaped out and bit down into my arm with all of his strength! He clamped on with the power of a vise-grip for several seconds before he decided to retract his fangs from my flesh. Immediately after he let go and dropped to the floor, he took several swipes with his razor sharp claws, carving out my legs before scurrying away.

As blood trickled out of my open wound, I was shocked! I burst into tears saying I didn't need this and I definitely was going to be late for work! My arm reacted to the deep bite with excruciating pain and swelling. I did my best to clean up my wound by disinfecting it and wrapping it in a sterile bandage.

I arrived at work several minutes late. After sitting down at my desk, I called Bry to tell him what happened. He told me I needed to have my arm checked out by a doctor in order to make sure it wasn't infected. I told him I was going to be fine and not to worry about it.

Throughout the workday, my arm hurt more and more. With increasing painful swelling, I was alarmed to see a visible red line creeping up my arm under the skin. The pain was unbearable and I knew an infection was spreading. By midday, I became nervous and extremely concerned about my rapidly deteriorating condition.

I called Bry again with an update. He said he was going to drive by and pick me up from work immediately! "We're going to urgent care and get this thing looked at!" Bryan arrived not too long after our chat and drove us towards our local urgent care center. As soon as the attending doc at the UC center saw my arm, he said it was a good thing I came in. My arm was seriously infected, and things would have deteriorated fast if I delayed treatment.

My doctor asked when I received my last tetanus shot. I said I had one as a child. "Okay," he said, "we're going to give you a tetanus and antibacterial shot. I'll call your pharmacy where you can pick up your antibacterial pills. Take them every day for the next 10 days straight."

$260.00 later, we were at home with my antibacterial pills waiting for Pat. On the way back from urgent care, I told her what happened. During our conversation, I told her she had to get her cats. After her ceremony, she immediately rushed over to pick up her "sweethearts." She wasn't happy, but I refused to stay with them another day!

When Pat didn't show any concern about my injuries and medical treatment, I became angry. She didn't apologize for the disaster, but was annoyed about us messing up her special day. She quickly found a friend to take her cats for the next couple of days. Pat ended up paying me $75.00 of the $150.00 dollars, but at least I had my apartment back. With money and time lost, I vowed to stop kitty sitting.

Laying in bed that night nursing my bandaged arm, I couldn't help but think, "Maybe I should consider sitting for pet rocks next time. At least they won't bite."

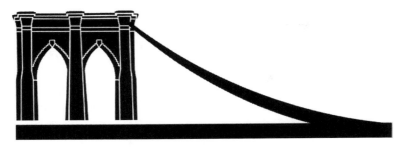

Chapter 6
The Norwegian Forest

After the mayhem with Max and his mates, a year went by without hearing from Jose and the kitty kennel place. It was fine by me; I wasn't interested in cat-sitting again.

One day I received a call from Jose and said he had the perfect cat-sitting job. I was about to tell him I wasn't interested until he mentioned the cash offer. The owners were moving back to Japan. They needed time to resolve quarantine and paperwork issues just like what happened with Toraji. This family was affluent and willing to pay handsomely for me to watch their 5 year-old Norwegian Forest cat. This gig was planned for the next five and a half months.

I met the family and their cat at a hotel in lower Manhattan where they stayed. Henry was an absolute darling! He was chilled out, peaceful, and sweet. His owners were nice too. By the end of our meeting, I agreed to take care of Henry. His owners and I signed our contract and scheduled a drop-off date. Bry wasn't pleased with our new venture after our past experience with Max, but Henry was super sweet and he'd love him.

A few days later, Henry the cat was delivered to our Brooklyn apartment. Because of dense traffic conditions, poor kitty had a bad case of motion sickness from the long taxi ride from downtown Manhattan. He threw up and pooped all over himself and his owner Kristen. When they arrived in our building's lobby, I came down with baby wipes to clean him off as much as possible. Our lobby's polished floor was smeared with his mess and needed a wipe down too.

Henry was brought upstairs for a shower and he was not happy. Kristen his owner needed a shower too so I supplied her with fresh clothes for her ride back home. Soon, we had Henry and his owner cleaned up.

Later, we sat down to discuss his feeding schedule and other details. Kristen had a collection of cute clothes for Henry to wear. I thought this was strange because Norwegian Forest cats are covered in puffy dense fur. I asked Kristen if the clothes were to keep him warm. She informed me the outfits were for her. Good, I thought... because I wasn't playing dress-up with this guy!

If you've never met Norwegian Forest cats, they're built like tanks. Henry's paws were nearly two inches wide and was a 25-pound lean, mean, Norwegian fighting machine! Bryan and I joked about posting a sign on our apartment door with, "Beware of the Norwegian Forest Cat." Thank God he was so sweet because if he was nasty like Max, he could've maimed or killed someone.

Bry didn't trust Henry, but this cat was precious. He was very affectionate, but on his cat terms. He'd let you know when he wanted some lovin', and he'd make it clear when to leave him alone. As long as you respected his boundaries, he was great to live with.

I grew to love Henry and secretly hoped his owners wouldn't come back for him. Unlike Torji, who strangely loved to be petted hard, Henry preferred to be touched lightly. Once I patted his head firmly like you would do to a dog and Henry looked at me like, "What was that? You better not do that again!" I got the message. Usually, we did the most cuddling right when I got home. He'd purr, and I'd hold him for a bit until he jumped out of my hands as if to say, "That's it! Time for eats."

One Saturday, Bry and I were away most of the day. When we came home, we found Henry in the foyer parked next to our apartment's door. He refused to let us in. Henry leaned and pressed his huge muscular body into our legs blocking us from entering the apartment. At first, we had no idea why Henry was acting this way until we got a whiff of poopy smell. Lo and behold, we looked at Henry's butt and saw he had a massive dingleberry hanging out! Henry was a very clean cat, and he hated being dirty. Once we noticed the problem, I scooped him up and brought him to our shower to clean him up. We knew he hated showers, but this time... he was super compliant and let me wash him.

Five and a half months with Henry the cat passed quickly and it was an emotional reunion when his owners returned to get him. I loved their kitty and I was going to miss him. Henry looked at me with those big soulful eyes probably wondering why he couldn't stay forever. I whispered to him, "I'll miss you, big guy. Don't hurt the customs agents at the airport." Since Kristen was with her mom for the pickup, we hugged and gave our tearful final goodbyes.

Our strong, but gentle giant departed our little New York home... never to return. Henry flew over most of North America and part of the mighty Pacific Ocean towards Japan, leaving a Norwegian Forest cat-sized hole in our hearts.

Chapter 7
Fur-ever Friend

After Henry the cat's departure, I was determined to have my first dog as an adult. When I was a child, our family had several dogs over the years. As an adult, I never owned one. During my 20's I traveled a bunch and couldn't take proper care of a furry buddy back then. Now I was jazzed and ready to find a forever doggie companion.

I checked the local animal shelters each week for available dogs. In particular, I was hoping to rescue a Yorkie. If I adopted a young dog and not a pup, he wouldn't be at risk of having health issues. At the same time, he'd be potty trained. Since I worked in Manhattan and commuted back-n-forth to Brooklyn by subway, I was usually away 10 or more hours. A dog small enough not requiring much space and attention would be relatively comfortable in my tiny apartment.

Bry wasn't a big fan of having a dog join our pack. As a child, his family dogs always lived in the backyard in their own doggie house his dad built. Dogs weren't meant to be indoors from his perspective.

During the following weeks, I checked the online animal shelters every day to see what breeds were available. Most of the rescues were big dogs like Rottweilers and Pit Bulls. I had no space for a dog this big. The moment a small dog was available, I rushed over to the shelter. By the time I got there, the small dogs were snatched up. It was so frustrating, but the caretaker said this was normal because most people in the city wanted small dogs.

After two months, I was starting to get discouraged and thought I'd never find my forever doggie. One day at work towards the end of the day I read a new post. It showed two puppy Yorkies were recently up for adoption at a nearby shelter. I couldn't wait for the next hour to end so I could run over and hopefully take one of these guys home with me. I didn't want a puppy, but given how hard it was to get any small dog, I was ready to make exceptions. Unfortunately, by the time I arrived at the shelter, both dogs were snatched up! I was so discouraged.

I asked the service director if there were any small dogs available. She showed me two dogs. One was a baby Pit Bull and the other, a Jack Russell Terrier who seemed really unfriendly and loud. I knew he wouldn't be a good fit for us. Our neighbors in our building would be forced to suffer through the echoes of constant barking.

When I was about to turn and leave, I spotted a small black mutt of a dog in a glass cage by himself. He wasn't the cute Yorkie I originally planned on getting, but this one was handsome! Through his glass cage, I saw him sitting on his makeshift doggie bed wearing a knitted sweater shaking a small plush toy in his mouth. I stopped the service director and asked, "What about him?" She said he wasn't ready for adoption because he was a new arrival and needed to be checked out to make sure he was healthy enough for adoption.

I begged her to let me see him. She stepped away for a moment and when she came back, she said I could see him. If I was interested, I could place a deposit. If he became adoptable, they'd give me a call. If he wasn't healthy enough to adopt, they'd put him down. Because of this, I wouldn't get my deposit back. I was willing to take the risk!

When this Manhattan shelter, which was a short 30 minute train ride away from Brooklyn brought him in, he didn't have any tags. He was found abandoned somewhere within the Upper East Side of Manhattan. The nice peeps at the animal shelter named him Fred. He was a Lhasa Apso/Poodle mix at about 13 pounds. Fred was terribly underweight by about 6 pounds. He was so skinny, his spine was clearly visible after all of his matted and severely knotted hair was shaved off right down to his skin.

Fred was a little apprehensive and somewhat nervous when they carried him over to me for the first time. The shelter's handler assumed he was a companion of an elderly tenant who died in an old apartment building. Fred was left alone and forced to survive without food and water. He was dirty and in a filthy mess because of the bathroom thing. It was possible a superintendent didn't want to deal with the dog so he just threw him out into the street to survive on his own.

I was told Fred was super friendly to all humans, but scared of other dogs. We spent about 15 minutes getting acquainted when she briefed me about a few important things I needed to know. This shelter wanted to be sure I was okay with his unique characteristics before they considered me as a potential adopter of this little guy.

In addition to being friendly, Fred was potty trained. I was also warned about his very mouthy tendencies. He loved chewing on things... including your fingers and hands. It was his way of being affectionate. I wasn't worried about it and said this was okay with me. Given the trauma this little guy suffered and endured, they wanted to be sure Fred wasn't abandoned again. They told me if things did not work out, please... without hesitation bring him back so they could match him with an appropriate family. I confidently told them it wouldn't be a problem. Fred definitely had a forever home with me!

After saying, See ya later, Fred," the shelter's assistant walked me out of the holding area. I was told they'd contact me within the next couple of weeks when or if Fred was ready for adoption. I was confident all would work out!

Immediately, when I got back to Brooklyn, I prepared our humble tiny abode for our new furry friend's greatly anticipated arrival. I bought several outfits for him and picked up a bunch of doggie toys. Included in Fred's homecoming package was a water and food bowl, a doggie bed, collar and leash, and a doggie carrier. Of course, I couldn't forget about stocking up on poop bags!

Three weeks later on a Wednesday morning, I got the call from the shelter. Fred was ready and available for pickup. They would hold him for the next 24 hours, so I better come in and get him now. Woohoo!

The night prior to pickup, I had a nasty tummy-ache with frequent bathroom visits. I called out sick next day from work. Since I was so excited Fred was ready, I was a little concerned about the subway ride to the shelter without any incidents. Thinking about getting stuck in the tunnels for any delays ramped up my stress levels. Avoiding a catastrophe, I skipped breakfast, brought some water, and ran towards the station to ride the Manhattan-bound R train to pick up my new fur buddy.

Thankfully, I arrived at the shelter without incident. As soon as I walked inside the building and made my way towards reception, I was ready to complete the adoption process. With nervous excitement, I filled out and signed the required adoption paperwork; it didn't take long. Within 30 minutes, a handler brought Fred out to me.

Upon making contact, she was shocked when she saw I had a doggie carrier, outfits, and a leash with me. She said this wasn't the norm since most people came in with nothing. The shelter's veterinarian gave me some tips and advice on canine care and feeding. They blessed Fred and I with a care-package of one huge bag of food and doggy treats for the next month. I was super proud to leave the shelter with my spiffy and handsome Lhasa.

As we left the shelter, I remembered my best friend worked a couple of blocks from there. I wanted to drop by and show off my new fur man. I gave her a call and she said to come right over. My friend and all of her co-workers loved Fred! They played with him for 45 minutes and proceeded to share the many snacks the shelter gave us. My friend asked if we'd be taking a cab home. I told her I planned to take the train back to Brooklyn. My friend said, no! She handed me some money and said, "Take a car service; it'll be less stressful for him." I thanked her, walked out, waited for the car, and rode home.

During the cab ride, Fred sat proudly smiling in my lap. When we entered the building, rode the elevator up, and walked through the doorway of our tiny apartment, he immediately ran to his new doggie bed. Inside his bed was a new owl toy. He grabbed it with his mouth and aggressively shook it back and forth. It made a crispy crunchy sound when it was tossed around. Fred was so grateful to be in his new forever home!

Lying in bed during the middle of the night, Fred jumped on my chest and vomited on me. From the stress of the day and many doggy snacks, including a car ride home, my new friend was overwhelmed. Welcome to pet ownership!

Next day, Bry came home. He was not impressed with our new addition, saying, "Are you sure you want this one? He is not handsome." I told him, for health and hygienic reasons the shelter shaved Fred's body down to his skin, even his boney tail. His tail looked like a rat's tail which was unattractive. I knew his hair would grow out and he'd be super handsome, but my honey disagreed.

During the next few days, Bry and I discussed possible new names for Fred. According to the shelter, they said he was rescued without tags and just named him Fred. Since our new buddy didn't look like a Fred to us, we wanted a change.

Initially, when I considered getting a Yorkie, I thought about naming my new pup Piper. Piper was an airplane I loved flying during Private Pilot flight training and it was my favorite; but Fred didn't seem like a Piper.

A few days later one evening, I called out to Fred, but accidentally called him Henry. Since Henry the cat flew to Japan about a month ago, his name was still fresh in my mind. I shouted Henry instead of Fred. The odd thing was, our new doggy naturally responded and immediately ran over to me when I called him Henry. Bryan joked and said, "What if he was named Henry by his previous owner?" We laughed in amazement and decided from that day forth, Fred's new name was to be "Henry Frederick Hobbs!" Frederick was in honor and remembrance of the name the animal shelter gave him. Hobbs was given to him after the Hobbs meter in an aircraft because we wanted an aviation-related component to Henry's new name.

After writing this book, our dear Henry has been with us for eight and a half glorious years! Henry was, is, and will continue being a true blessing to our family. He even served as our Best Man at our wedding in Manhattan.

It's pretty cool knowing my quest for a cute Yorkie lead us to a handsome, charcoal-colored, shaggy, little Lhasa Apso mutt with a heart of gold named Henry Frederick Hobbs! Life sure has its funny ways of working out.

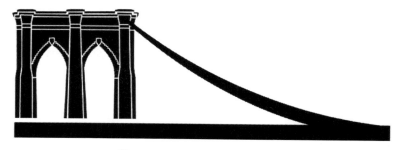

Chapter 8
Thousand-dollar Scone

After Henry Hobbs arrived in our tiny Brooklyn apartment, the first couple of weeks were a true gettin'-to-know-ya phase. We were all figuring each other out; it was like moving in with a new roomie during our first awkward and sometimes challenging moments living together.

A few weeks in, one of Bry's HDMI cables conveniently became Henry's doggie chew-toy of the day. Bryan was not thrilled. Making matters worse, one evening we came home and found strange burn marks on our hardwood living room floor. While we wondered why the black scars were there, we saw our RC quad-copter's battery cracked open. Again, Henry decided to gnaw through something he shouldn't have. We assumed he dropped the battery as soon as he felt a zap in his mouth. After this shocking event, you better believe we made sure our place was safe for us and our friend. Knowing how close we came to experiencing a potential apartment fire was sobering. Thank God... Henry was okay! He was just too curious for his own good.

Bry, in his signature deadpan way muttered, "This isn't going to work," implying Henry might be pawing his way back to the doggie pound. Regardless, since Henry was in a new home, I knew we needed just a little bit of time to figure things out. He was still trying to learn his boundaries and I was determined to make this work! I assured Bryan, as long as we kept things out of our fur-buddy's reach, we'd all be fine.

On a happier note, the tech company I worked for in Manhattan celebrated their dog-friendly policy on Fridays. Because of this, I brought Henry to the job once a month and he absolutely LOVED it! I carried in his comfy bed, toys, and lunch. Hen lounged quietly by my desk soaking in all of the attention from my coworkers. Throughout our workday, people stopped by to give him pets and treats. Henry basked in the spotlight of his newly found office-celebrity status.

During our "Friday Office Day" when pets came to have fun, our company offered a free early morning breakfast buffet for our coworkers. Henry really enjoyed the culinary part of this Friday adventure; who could blame him? My go-to treats were the colorful fruit salads, delicious Danish pastries, and those irresistible cinnamon scones. Mmm, just thinking about them makes my mouth water!

One Friday evening after we got home from work, Bry suggested we head out and hit our favorite Brooklyn pizza joint for slices and cocktails. "Absolutely," I eagerly said, as I relished the idea of chillaxing after a busy week on the job.

After pizza and a couple of chocolate martinis later, we returned home to a very happy Henry. He always greeted us at the door with an exuberant display of joy, presenting us with his chosen toy of the evening from his mountain of plush toys. Every time we walked in the apartment, he'd rush to his personal stash, dig around for the perfect one, and proudly present it to us with his tail wagging like crazy! Catching the toy in the air was his favorite game, and tonight was no exception.

After a few rounds of fetch, I noticed my bag was knocked to the floor. "Oh no," I thought; pastry crumbs were everywhere. "HENRY!!!" I screamed; as I felt a pang of disappointment. I was looking forward to eating that scone since I bagged it from my job's breakfast party. Oh well, my Saturday's breakfast scone was a bust. After a little more playtime, we got ready for bed and settled in for the night.

The next day, since it was Saturday, we slept in a bit. Even though it was the weekend, Henry was eager to start the day so we got up and got ready. After a bit of playtime with our fur buddy, I took Henry out for his walk and my usual Saturday morning coffee run. We weren't more than two blocks from our building when I felt a tug on Henry's leash and heard someone behind us shout, "WAIT!"

I quickly turned around to see what was happening and saw Henry vomiting. Oh great! I looked down to see what he threw up and saw something like a whole hotdog. Where on earth did he get that?! After a quick cleanup, we continued on to the coffee shop where I grabbed my usual hot cappuccino before returning to the apartment.

On the way back, Henry threw up twice more. By the time we got home, I figured he expelled whatever was bothering him. I told Bryan about what happened and had no idea what Hen ate which could've made him so sick. We were always careful about Henry's diet. He usually had dry kibble mixed in with wet food, chicken, and veggies.

Just as I was about to start recording my scheduled Saturday podcasts, Henry began throwing up blood! What the heck?! Panic set in as I shouted to Bry, "CALL THE VET!" I quickly contacted all my podcast guests to cancel their interviews and reschedule. I explained to them my dog was very sick. Thankfully, the vet's office was just a couple of blocks away from our pad. When we arrived at the pet clinic, they took us in immediately.

While in the facility, Henry threw up blood... twice! First episode was in the waiting room and the second one happened in the exam room... right in front of the doc. Hen's vet whisked him away for x-rays and gave him a shot to calm his stomach. Henry was trapped in a vicious cycle of acute spasmodic episodes of pain and blood.

A moment later, the doctor returned with Henry and his x-rays. On the video screen, the doc pointed out a half-eaten chew toy in Henry's stomach, but didn't think it was the cause of the excessive vomiting. During our conversation, he asked us to walk him through everything Henry ate within the past 24 to 48 hours.

As best as I could remember, I recited Hen's list of meals he ate. I also explained what happened Friday night when our pup ate the pastries. Our vet asked if any of the pastries had raisins. "Well... yes, the scone had raisins," I replied. "But that wouldn't make him sick, would it?" The doctor's facial expression quickly changed and turned serious. He explained raisins—and grapes—were highly toxic to dogs. My heart sank!

My veterinarian gave us a detailed list of foods to avoid and told us they'd keep Henry at the clinic to monitor him during his initial recovery. Fewer than 24 hours later we received a call and were cleared to pick up Henry. They sent us home with prescription meds to help Hen heal quickly and a variety of vet-approved food for the next two weeks.

This whole ordeal was stressful and... terrifying! Our beautiful doggie friend, this precious soul who recently entered into our lives, almost died.

In the end, that raisin scone which I never ate, turned out to be the most expensive tasty pastry of my life! It cost us over a thousand dollars for one terribly stressful, unforgettable veterinarian visit.

Thank God... our sweet little Henry pulled through and was back to his friendly, playful, loving self in no time.

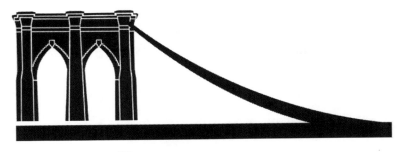

Chapter 9
Cappuccino Chronicles

My friends and co-workers know I'm a big fan of cappuccinos. During my teens and young adult life, my friends called me a tea snob. Since I found the taste of coffee too bitter, I drank loads of tea and was extremely particular about buying high-end exotic teas until one evening at a friend's house.

While visiting my friend, I smelled a heavenly aroma. I asked her what she was making, and replied with, "Ponche." This hot beverage consisted of egg whites, chocolate cocoa powder, evaporated milk, and Café Bustelo espresso. She simmered the ingredients for a good long while and served the drink to her kids after dinner.

I couldn't take it anymore and asked if I could have some of this Ponche. She obliged and gave me a small cup. WOW, this was the most amazing drink I ever had! I was tempted to ask for another, but held back. A couple of days later while out with a friend for brunch, I told her about this new heavenly drink I recently had. She told me,

"You might want to try a chocolate cappuccino. It's frothy and would have the same dessert consistency." I figured, what the heck, and ordered a mocha cappuccino.

This cappuccino wasn't as good as the Ponche, but it was a very close second, so I ordered another one. From my 30's onward my drink of choice each morning, and many afternoons, were chocolate or mocha capps!

Living in the vibrant borough of Brooklyn, I was spoiled with access to an abundance of wonderful cafés and coffee joints. I became painfully particular about how I wanted my capps crafted. They were foamy and very, very strong! Shortly after moving to Bay Ridge, Brooklyn, a nearby coffee joint became my daily hotspot for cappuccinos and weekend brunches. There were many regulars who patronized the joint each weekend just like the television show, Cheers. Everyone knew each other's names.

We shared chats as we sipped our delicious hot coffees over plates of tasty edibles. One guy was a huge pancake fan. He'd bring his own natural Vermont syrup to pour over his freshly made hotcakes. The owners of this joint was a couple my husband dubbed as Fred and Wilma from the show, The Flintstones.

Fred worked and managed his café every day of the week. One weekend, he became annoyed when I said I wished the weekends lasted longer. He firmly replied with, "At least you get a break. I've been running this place for more than 20 years working seven days a week." I asked him why he didn't hire help? Fred said he and his wife tried that years ago, but had issues with employee theft and incompetent management. Fred had a point.

Some people seem to think business owners have it easy. A business operator may be able to properly staff and equip his establishment, but all responsibilities fall squarely on the shoulders of the owner... whether he's on scene or not. With clock-punchers, employees can walk away from the job at quitting time and not think about work until the next day. Owning a business is a full time job, 24-7-365.

Fred and Wilma created and maintained an incredible business environment. Customers were able to meet and connect with wonderful neighbors who shared countless amazing conversations over the years. After year seven, I noticed Fred was overwhelmed with his business-related stress.

Multiple incidents led me to stop patronizing their place. One such event occurred during one of my weekend brunches. Wilma noticed I usually ordered two mocha capps for brunch and suggested I order their large mocha capp. "What?! I didn't know you sold large mocha cappuccinos." Wilma said, "We do, but it's only available on our to-go menu, since we don't stock 16 oz. mugs. If you don't mind drinking out of a paper cup, I'll give you the large. This option will save you $3.00." I replied with, "Wow, that will work, thanks!"

For the next couple of weekends, I continued ordering the large paper cup of coffee. One day Fred stopped Wilma as she steam-foamed my capp, saying, "What are you doing?" "Large cups are for our to-go orders only!" She explained to him I always ordered two small capps every weekend and suggested I order the large since it approximated two small cups. Fred was upset and said if I wanted the large, I had to take my coffee to go. "Okay, I'll order two small cups to stay, but could I get three dollars off my two capps?" My ask was met with a resounding, "No!"

Wow, I was extremely sad. As a patron for over seven years, I felt Fred's uncompromising and unaccommodating stance was a complete diss. He had no appreciation for all of the money I spent over the years at his restaurant. Since this experience, many regulars stopped coming by, including me.

After leaving Fred and Wilma's spot, I discovered a new coffee joint which opened a block over. Yay! There was one thing which made this new café better; the owner allowed me to bring my new fur buddy Henry into his establishment. I wasn't too comfortable eating inside with Henry, but at least I could enter the shop to order my capp without resistance before starting my morning walk with my friend.

Sadly, this new joint didn't last long. During the shop's short run, I quickly became friends with the workers. They shared stories of the horrible abuses they faced from the owner of this cute coffee bar. As a result, I went to another coffee bar near the R subway station where I rode the train to work each morning.

At the subway café, their service was also horrendous! Workers at this place suffered through worse abuse from the shop owner. This jerk of an owner didn't even hide his disdain and disrespect aimed at his workers. He often yelled and cursed at them in front of his customers. No one should have to put up with that abuse and behavior. Seriously, what the heck is wrong with these people?!

This subway café stirred up horrible memories of an early position I had working for a company in my 20's. My old boss was the owner of a small business. He made a point each day to make at least one of us in the office cry. It was a terrible place to work!

Years earlier when I first moved to Bay Ridge, I went to a café a block from me. I tried their espresso and wasn't a fan of it, but I decided to give them another try. This café was quaint and tastefully decorated with eclectic furniture. Boy was I glad to give them a second chance because their capps were amazing! They sold mostly lattes, cappuccinos, assorted French press coffees, and fresh pastries, including a few pre-made sandwiches. Best part was their exceptional customer service! This place became my coffee hangout for the next several years until we moved away from Brooklyn.

What impressed me the most about this fine joint, besides their great food and drinks, was how the storekeepers really went out of their way to make me feel special. This small coffee bar became an oasis for many, including myself. It was run by two sisters who always made sure they found a solution which made their customers happy. I sincerely appreciated it!

I remember one beautiful sunny day, Bry and I sat at one of their outdoor tables when a bird flew by and dropped an aerial poop bomb on our table. One of the sisters saw what happened and apologized. She ordered the staff to get me a new cappuccino and new pastry. While waiting for our food and drinks to arrive, they moved us to a clean table. Now that's great service!

Additionally, Henry and I enjoyed many wonderful weekend muffins and cappuccinos at this fine neighborly Bay Ridge café! When it came to coffee and tasty cappuccinos, it wasn't just about the drinks, it was about a great experience. Sometimes, a little bit of bird poop was just part of the excitement!

Here's to finding your perfect cup o' Joe. May your favorite baristas always be as enthusiastically delightful as mine!

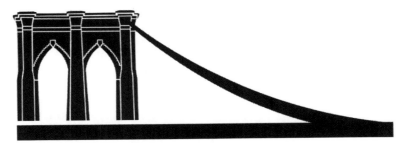

Chapter 10
Snowed-in Smart Summer Ale

I generally shopped on Saturday afternoons for groceries. One freezing mid-winter afternoon, I looked through my window and saw an insane amount of snow covering our streets. It snowed heavily from an unusually strong Nor'easter which passed over the city during the night. This storm dumped over two feet of crystallized precipitation which paralyzed New York for a few days. NYC always had snowfalls, but this event was extremely rare. It was so rare, we heard thunder and saw a few flashes of lightning. We called it, thunder-snow.

Ack, how could I ever get my groceries home?! I usually took my granny cart and walked nine blocks to and from our local supermarket. With deep snow everywhere, it wasn't happening. I wondered if the store was making deliveries. Could I grab a cab? I better get cracking to see what options I had.

When I walked through our building's courtyard after the snowfall, I looked at our teeny-tiny smart car parked at the corner of our block. It was buried under what looked like five feet of snow! When DSNY (Dept. of Sanitation) rolled their huge plow-blades connected to heavy garbage trucks, they pushed and piled a mountain of snow against our smart. Wow, how could we ever dig out our ride?

In Bay Ridge, Brooklyn, temps were hanging around 18 degrees Fahrenheit! It was a freezing and windy afternoon. With ice forming a hard shell, it would've taken hours of exhaustive shoveling to get our car out from under the snow and ice. Just as I was thinking about how we'd dig our car out, I noticed a huge orange Sanitation Dept. front-loader clearing snow. It was carving a path through a massive pile which was obstructing the Catholic school's driveway across the street. At that moment, I had a great idea!

I walked up to the plow-operator and told him my tiny smart car was buried under loads of snow across the street. I asked if he'd accept a cash tip and dig out most of the snow around our car. He explained he worked for the city and couldn't accept my money, but after he finished plowing the street around the school, he'd see what he could do. I thanked him, walked away, and headed over to my local supermarket.

When I arrived at the market, they were open for business and sending deliveries out. After an hour of shopping, I pushed my full cart towards checkout. An announcement came through the speakers saying all further deliveries were canceled for the day. Oh no, there was no way I could get these items home! I left my spot in line to track down the manager. All of the staff at this location knew me, so I explained my situation. There was no way I could get my groceries home without a store delivery. I asked if there was any way they could make an exception. The manager yelled over to my cashier and instructed her to schedule my delivery and tag me as the last outgoing for the day. I saw angry glances as I walked back to my cart.

After navigating through deep snow and carefully treading on icy sidewalks, I finally arrived in front of my building. Before going upstairs to wait for my groceries to be delivered, I saw our smart across the street. WOW, the plow guy almost completely dug our car out! This was a blessing! In most cases I wouldn't bother asking for help; but on that day I asked two people for help and got a yes on both asks. We won't always get a positive response in the affirmative, but if we don't ask, we won't get. The worst anyone could say to our ask is, "No!"

A couple of months later, warm weather began creeping in. It was early May and we were heading out to pick up food for the week. Bry mentioned, "I think Samuel Adams Summer Ale is available in May. When we get to the store, let's check if there's any in stock."

Bry rarely went in the store with me to shop, but waited in the car with our doggy buddy, Henry. I entered the supermarket and quickly selected the items we needed. Just as I was about to check out, I remembered Bry's favorite ale. I walked towards the beverage aisle and scanned the wide selection of beers and ales. Unfortunately, I didn't see Samuel Adams.

Oh well, I tried. Walking over to the cashiers, I spotted Cindy, a store clerk. "Hey Cindy, how are you? I was hoping you could find something for me."

"Yeah, sure," she said. "What's up?"

"Do you have any Samuel Adams Summer Ale in stock? I looked for it in the beer aisle, but didn't see any. Do you have any cases in the back?"

"I'll check," Cindy said.

While Cindy was in the back, I grabbed a couple of last-minute items and returned to the help desk. A few minutes later, Cindy came over and cheerily said they didn't have any Summer Ale in storage, but inventory was expecting a delivery later in the week. "Great! Thank you, Cindy," I said while enthusiastically giving her two thumbs up.

It was then when I took a quick glance at my two hands and realized with horror I didn't give Cindy two thumbs up, but... two middle fingers!

I quickly and awkwardly corrected it with the proper thumbs-up and profusely apologized!

Cindy was bubbling with uncontrollable laughter, and so was I! For the next five minutes we couldn't catch our breath as we laughed to the point of tears! I'm not sure how I made this crazy mistake, but every time we saw each other at the supermarket, we'd burst out laughing. Thank God she was cool in understanding my humorously embarrassing gaffe. As a result, we remained friends.

This was a moment for another valuable lesson learned. Always be ready to laugh at yourself; it's the best way to turn a crazy awkward moment into a hilariously funny memory!

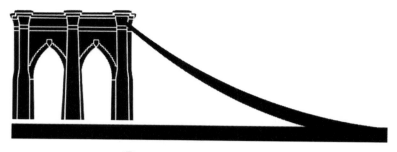

Chapter 11
Brooklyn Heights, Texas Delights

This Brooklyn neighborhood was a hidden gem buried within the midst of an old gritty city when we first moved in. Our historic apartment building was by far the coolest and nicest place to live in during my entire adult life in New York.

When we first arrived, all of our neighbors knew each other and looked out for one another. This was the way old school New Yorkers rolled back in the day. No matter where we came from, we had each other's back. It was peaceful in our part of Bay Ridge and our building. We were near shops, restaurants, grocery stores, parks, and schools. The massive towers of the Verrazano-Narrows Bridge were always visible during the day and spectacularly illuminated with sparkling strings of light at night. Also, New York harbor was a brief walk away where we'd gaze over the dark blue water watching heavy ships cruise inbound and out. As if I had to mention, lower Manhattan was clearly visible from our special hangout spot with its densely packed skyscrapers reaching for the urban sky.

However, in recent years with the sale of the building to a new owner, old tenants moved out and new ones moved in. As a result, less-than-ideal neighbors were arriving on scene. Domestic issues began manifesting with NYPD being called for service. Drug use and indecent behavior slowly crept in.

One incident, a crack smoker was caught toking on a pipe in the stairwell. Another time, two neighbors were getting it on hot-n-heavy in another stairwell. What happened to our beautiful peaceful urban abode? Was the honeymoon ending? Where did the warmth and wonder go? This was definitely not a special place to live in any longer.

In fact, after new management took over, they told all tenants they had to remove their air-conditioner units from the windows. This was so outrageous, they had to be kidding us?! We were about to enter summertime and this old NYC building wasn't equipped with central air-conditioning. How were we going to combat the urban heat and mugginess? Our new management office sent out flyers warning tenants about mandatory air-conditioner removal from all windows. They said the building was in violation of FDNY fire regulations. Non-compliance of window-unit removal would not be tolerated, especially the units installed near the fire escape.

We knew management was dead wrong about this! So Bry, being a guy from The Bronx, wasn't taking this jab lying down! He carefully looked up codes and regulations from the NYC Dept. of Buildings and FDNY fire codes. He found, as long as an apartment with a fire escape had more than one window egress in the room with the AC unit, there was no violation.

Since our living room had two side-by-side windows facing the fire escape, both windows offered emergency egress. If one of those two living room windows was occupied with our air conditioner, then our apartment wasn't in violation. On the other hand, if there was only one window in that room with access to the fire escape, then we couldn't legally block that window.

Bryan was kind enough to print out multiple copies of the official documents he found online. Several key pages were highlighted pointing out important regulatory references. After that, we handed them to our elderly neighbors in our building. We armed them with information they could stand on if the super and landlord got dumb! We were especially concerned about what could happen during severe summer temperatures if these tenants didn't have their air conditioners installed.

During the following weeks, management became tyrannically aggressive by removing and confiscating AC units from all of the apartments. They had the nerve taking units from the elderly tenants too. For some reason, our place was last on their list.

Later, I expected a knock on our apartment door from the super. One day he knocked and I answered. He told me he'd come back with someone to remove our AC unit from the window. I aggressively replied with, "No you won't! You wanna come in here and take my stuff, you better get a warrant!" I showed the super the papers proving our unit wasn't in violation of any NYC codes.

Because of our building's downward slide during the past couple of years, we had our locks changed. Since this was the case, there was no way these guys could get into our apartment and steal our AC while we were out!

Staying armed with proper information and standing strong within our rights paid off big time! We never complied nor cooperated with management's foolishness and our super couldn't do anything about it. They didn't dare bring up the subject of removing our unit ever again!

Our neighbors were furious! They said it was completely unfair their units were taken away and ours were not. I reminded them, what the landlord did was completely against the law and in criminal violation of our Constitutional 4th Amendment right! Our tenants were never in violation of anything. They unlawfully entered, stole, and took possession of everyone's property!

Bit by bit, neighbors went out and replaced their stolen AC units. While this happened, I wondered what management did with the tenants' stolen property. Did they sell them on eBay or install them in the windows of their other buildings? We never found out.

Again, this incident reminded me we shouldn't allow anyone, including the government, to take advantage of us! No one is going to fight for us if we don't stand up for ourselves! If my husband didn't research, study, and understand New York's codes, statutes, and laws, I might have done what our neighbors did by giving into management's unlawful and unreasonable demands.

One afternoon, a few months later, we decided to hang out at our historic Brooklyn Heights and Brooklyn Promenade. The Prom, as we locals called it, was an elevated pedestrian shelf suspended above the BQE (Brooklyn Queens Expressway). Visitors from around the world would meet at this historic hotspot to view the stunning Manhattan skyline from across the southern end of the East River.

Hanging out at The Prom during a golden sunset and at night was extra special! Seeing and admiring the view of lower Manhattan's towering buildings, the nautical action along the river, the Verrazano-Narrows Bridge aka the VZ, and spotting our wonderful gift from the French in the harbor, our Statue of Liberty, was always a thrill!

Afterward, we'd walk down Henry Street to stop by one of the trendy local restaurants for some kick butt Italian cuisine. During dinner we got to talking, and I told Bry, Brooklyn Heights should be our next move. Over the next few months, Bryan and I went each weekend to The Heights to scope out the neighborhood. We completely fell in love with this area and decided to rent an Airbnb during spring for a week so we could get a boots-on-the-ground feel for living there. We knew living in this swanky area would mean paying way more for rent.

One afternoon, Bry and I had a Zoom chat with our friend Doc in Texas. We told him we were thinking of moving and loved Brooklyn Heights, but weren't sure we could swing the rent in the area. My friend immediately suggested we consider... Texas! "You'd get much more for your dollar here, plus there's no state tax requirement." Hmmm, interesting, I thought. We chatted a bit longer before saying our goodbyes. When we got off the phone, Bry and I started looking at houses near my friend from the Lone Star state. There were 4-bedroom houses for $250K and he was right! These houses would be close to 1 million dollars in New York City.

We liked the houses we checked out, but Bry wasn't about to move to the Midwest. He was born on The Rock, aka Manhattan and grew up within the trenches of the hardened Boogie Down Bronx of the 70's and 80's! This NYC boy definitely didn't see himself movin' outta town!

That all changed several months later when Covid, political riots, fires, vandalism, lockdowns, economic uncertainty, and fear settled within the big cities. This fear gripped the entire United States and the globe; but the inner cities, being way more congested, experienced greater tension.

It was March of 2020 when I finally convinced Bry to fly out to meet my friend in Texas. Doc planned to show us around town and introduce us to the rich Texas culture and way of life when we arrived. Experiencing a Texas rodeo was high on our agenda since it was in season during March. Unfortunately, most of Houston was on lockdown! Despite all that mess going on, we were still able to visit properties in the area and walk through several apartments. At one point we managed to shoot semi-auto pistols and a full-auto rifle at an extremely popular downtown shooting range! Yee-haw!

Most of my adult life I lived in small NYC apartments. It was such a refreshing breath of air seeing apartments with spacious rooms and luxurious amenities like private pools, gyms, and coffee bars. Was I on tour of a western heaven? Enjoying similar amenities in New York would require us to earn at least twice the income.

Texas reminded me of my childhood in Virginia, a place much friendlier than the inner city grit of the five boroughs. When 8 million breathing souls were smashed together, being suspicious and cautious of those hustling around you was the name of the game.

Several months later after flying back from Houston, we were driving away from our old New York friend, The Big Apple. We were packed and driving West towards the American heartland in a loaded moving truck with our good buddy, Henry. Our new destination was the great state of Texas! It was a bitter sweet moment, but we chose wisely. We were happy to be finally settled in our new home when we arrived. Today, Henry loves his aerial view from his lofty balcony!

What I missed most about living in NYC were my friends. To me, home was where my family was. Ever since I traded the hustle-n-bustle of big city life for the wide-open spaces of Texas, it was nice not worrying about stairwell crack-heads, risqué hallway romances, and crowded subway cars during rush hour.

I'm grateful for the memorable NYC experiences and wonderful people I met and knew within the best borough of New York, BROOKLYN!

My husband disagrees and reminds me with, "The Bronx is in da house!"

Here's to blazing trails with new Texas experiences without having to dig out a frozen smart car from under five feet of snow... ever again!

Fuggedaboudit!